THIS BOOK BELONGS TO:

....

....

Christmasland

ReCollections

RALPH DEL POZZO AND DAVID HIGH

COLLINS | DESIGN

An Imprint of HarperCollinsPublishers

HarperCollins books may be purchased for educational, business, or sales promotional use.
For information, please write: Special Markets Department, HarperCollins*Publishers*,
10 East 53rd Street, New York, NY 10022.

First Edition

First published in 2006 by:
Collins Design
An Imprint of HarperCollins*Publishers*
10 East 53rd Street
New York, NY 10022
Tel: (212) 207-7000
Fax: (212) 207-7654
collinsdesign@harpercollins.com
www.harpercollins.com

Distributed throughout the world by:
HarperCollins*Publishers*
10 East 53rd Street
New York, NY 10022
Fax: (212) 207-7654

Designed and photographed by Ralph Del Pozzo and David High
High Design, Inc.,140 Charles Street, No. 14A, New York, NY 10014
www.highdzn.com

Library of Congress Control Number: 2006921712

ISBN-10: 0-06-115000-2
ISBN-13: 978-0-06-115000-5

Manufactured in China
1 2 3 4 5 6 7 / 11 10 09 08 07 06 05
First Printing, 2006

We would both like to thank everyone who gave us a pat on the back for our first book: know that your kind words and enthusiasm gave us the courage to do it all over again. Thanks to all the little elves over at Collins Design: Marta Schooler and Elizabeth Sullivan, for really pushing; Ilana Anger, Dinah Fried, and Margarita Vaisman, for keeping it all running smoothly; Paul Olsewski, for our 14 minutes; and Roni Axelrod, for producing such a beautiful package. Many thanks also to the Coxsackie Antiques Center and CYMK, Inc.

As we look forward to future holiday celebrations, we continue to cherish Christmases past. Looking back, one comes to realize that the best memories are comprised of very special people — our family and friends: the Balfes, Barbarisis, Colwells, Del Pozzos, Donahues, Dorr, Highs, Heddens, Hiller, Hundertmark, Husseys, Kaszluga, Kuntzmans, Lehs, Lefevers, Magees, Marcoletas, Meachers, Mcknight, Mitchinsons, Nordfors, Shannons, Sofield, Sullivans, and Schultise-Pearce.

thank You:

RALPH WOULD LIKE TO
DEDICATE THIS BOOK TO
HIS PARENTS:

Ralph and Nancy Del Pozzo

♥

DAVID WOULD LIKE TO
DEDICATE THIS BOOK TO
HIS PARENTS:

Robert and Arlene High

There is but a very brief window in early childhood for us all, a period of time that lasts from birth until we are cast from the nest and into school. A time when all about the world is new and good. A time when we are open. A time when we take things in so deeply that they will form us ever after. So we imprint upon the Christmas of that time, and what that was is what it will be for us always. That is what collecting is about: The power that an object unseen in decades can have to transport us in mind and spirit back to a specific period or moment of our lives — to unlock long-closed doors in the mansion of our memory — is the true value that it has. We can hold such an object in our hands and know those times were real, and welcome back whole parts of who we were into who we are — and let the inner child in each of us out to play again — to live as part of us and help us see again through our own Magic Window.

—Ted Althof, papatedsplace.com

Once

upon a time, Christmasland tableaux existed in great numbers within the houses that dotted the newly suburbanized landscapes across this great planet. There were no fast rules to follow, so they could appear in any number of niches or crannies: on top of the brand-new Magnavox television, across the faux-fireplace mantel, under the Christmas tree, even on the martini cart, right next to the shiny silver cocktail shaker. It was a chance to exercise creative freedom and let your imagination (and grouping skills) go wild, all the while sprinkling festive holiday cheer and ambience throughout the entire household (along with bags and bags of plastic snow and mica glitter).

Most likely the earliest developments to boom under the Christmas tree were brought about by model railroad cars and tracks, which started merely as a holiday hobby. The towns and villages that multiplied along the train's route soon blossomed with a number of unusual inhabitants — from plastic deer and chenille snowmen to pinecone elves brandishing about a multitude of musical instruments. The cardboard dwellings these creatures lived in were as diverse as the full-sized developments sprouting up in former cornfields. "Cocos" were covered in shredded cellophane, which gave them a stuccoed hacienda feel. "Lakkies" (slang for laquered) were unique, with their brilliant colors and high-gloss enameled look. "Printies" were covered in intricate lithographed patterns of brickwork, stone, curtains, and tiny window boxes, while the corrugated "loggies" possessed an Adirondack ambience all their own. From the golden age, 1928–1934, to the time they finally fell from vogue in the 1960s, the one unifying thread of the different phases of dime-store architecture was their transparent windows. The warm glow emanating from these portals would invariably beckon observers closer and closer, undeniably urging them to crawl into the warm, wonderful, and completely imaginary world within.

One of the earliest records of a decorated tree comes from the journal of an unnamed traveler who visited Strasbourg, France, in 1605: "At Christmastime fir trees are set up in rooms...and hung with roses cut from paper of many colors, apples, wafers, spangle-gold, and sugar. It is customary to surround it with a square frame." Most likely, the setup this guy described was a tabletop number surrounded by a fence, which was usually employed to enclose a small **WINTRY LANDSCAPE** within its tiny boundaries. This tradition continues well into the present, especially with the renewed interest in vintage German feather trees. Some of the earliest figures for these little snowy scenes were made from some sort of composite material or even unfired clay. Many did not hold up well, leaving behind only a pair of minuscule snowboot-clad feet on a cabin's front steps as evidence of their existence. The two little bambinos pictured here, however, are made out of solid lead and have held up quite well despite their considerable age.

PixieLand

Pixies,

sprites, and elves are all put to manual labor by Santa in some form or another, depending on their country of origin. They are basically interchangeable, although they do have their own subtle personality quirks and nuances. Danish children know them as *Juul Nisse* and believe they reside in the attics of their homes. Instead of leaving out cookies and glasses of milk on Christmas Eve, the kids leave bowls of rice pudding and saucers of milk for the creatures to lap from.

No vintage holiday collection is complete without a few thousand **PORCELAIN FIGURINES**. Christmas critters flooded the market from the 1940s to the 1960s and could take the form of anything from Santa's mischievous little helpers (pixies and elves) to carolers, choir children, angels, and pretty holiday shoppers. Although many of these masterpieces were created in Japan, the majority of the companies themselves began and remained based in America. Far too many existed to mention them all, but several stand out due to their wit, ingenuity, and the sheer numbers with which they infiltrate our collections. Abe Moses was one of the first to import ceramic collectibles from Japan in 1850 through his Louisiana-based company, Ucagco. In 1939, Murray Kreiss brought us Kreiss Company. He added glitter to the mix with the generous use of rhinestones (especially for glamorous gemlike eyes!) as well as holiday humor with the incomparable "Psycho-Santas." Josef Originals began as a hobby in the early 1940s by Meriel Josef George in California. Eventually, competition caused Meriel and her husband to manufacture in Japan, although they maintained the design studio here. Beryl Gilner started Gilner Potteries in California in 1948, and, after becoming inspired by the leprechauns of Ireland, the American pixie was born! One of our favorites, Holt Howard, began in 1949 in New York City. Besides oodles of witty holiday designs, you can also thank that company for creating the very first candle huggers. Lefton was based in Chicago, Napco in Ohio, and Ruben's in California. All of these companies, along with so many others, shared one common goal: to fill our hearts, minds, and countertops with lots of Little People!

CANDY CANES were originally straight sticks and completely white. Around the seventeenth century, Europeans began decorating their Christmas trees (a then-new addition to their holiday celebrations) with edible foods and candy. The choirmaster at Cologne Cathedral, Germany, is credited with being the first to curve the stick into its now-familiar shape to represent a shepherd's crook (most likely to hang easier as well). These little nuggets also proved especially valuable in keeping small children quiet and occupied during long holiday services. August Imgard, a German immigrant, is linked to the first historical reference of candy canes in America when he decorated his Wooster, Ohio, tree with them in 1847! Approximately fifty years later, candy canes started appearing on Christmas cards with their ubiquitous red stripes (cards prior to 1900 boasted only all-white canes). Shortly thereafter, peppermint and wintergreen flavors were added (previously they were left unflavored). Gregory Keller, a Catholic priest, invented the first automatic candy cane machine in the 1950s. The beauteous canes pictured here, however, came from Altamarie's Candies in Kingston, New York, where brothers Michael and Frank Briglia learned the lost art of creating candy canes entirely by hand from the company's founder, Michael Altamarie, who brought the wooden batch roller that is still in use from the Coney Island boardwalk in 1896. (The worker-elf was not included...we found him.)

ITEM NO. 7590
HANGING
MISTLETOE
DECORATIVE
BALL
CLUSTER
MADE IN U.S.A.
BY BRADFORD

It's all about finding
that perfect tree...

The Country Church
with candle light and chime bells

MEMORIES OF CHURCH have always been intertwined with the holidays for me (perhaps because it was the only time my mother could get us all to go, though she vehemently denies this). My father would don his self-made Christmas hat, complete with blinking battery-powered lights and ornaments that circled the brim and swung about like Minnie Pearl's price tag — but that sort of thing really wasn't very unusual for him. My mother, however, would metamorphose right before our very eyes by teasing the hair on top of her head really high, dabbing on some of her special Shalimar Eau de Toilette by Guerlain, and clasping on her charm bracelet that sounded like a million jingle bells. The icing on the cake was a pair of paste-pearl ball earrings that dangled glamorously on thin gold chains. She would also put on a very stern face and keep it there. Whenever my brother (who was very much older and should have known better) would start in on me during the service, she would swat us both lightly and give us her "look of annihilation and death." This happened *every* time we attended church. I remember thinking, "Where is my mother?" and "Who in the world is this mean, mean woman?" **-D**

WINDOW DECORATION

MANTEL DECORATION

SO MANY USES!

CHRISTMAS TREE-TOP

A NIGHT LIGHT

The true heyday of "Made in Japan" Christmas ceramicware was from the mid-1950s to the mid-1960s, petering out completely by the early 1970s. As the industry grew, manufacturers added time-consuming techniques such as starched-lace accents, flocking, and **SPAGHETTI TRIM** to set their ceramic bric-a-brac far apart from the competetion's. Sometimes drawing up their fanciful ideas right on the factory premises, American importers would enlist the help of interpreters to avoid any confusion. This little shopaholic, however, must have gotten lost in translation. Upon finding her, one can imagine the assembly line being told, "She needs big red tear ducts! Don't forget the big red tear ducts!" It is quirky culture gaps such as this that make these endearing trinkets so feverishly sought after in the first place.

This little gem is known throughout my family as "Grandpa's Angel." After her father's death in 1968, my mother bought four matching candle holders — each with its own muumuu-clad deity attached — for us, her mother, and her two brothers to light each Christmas in his memory. Years later, the angel was converted into an ornament, and it was always a huge deal when she was unpacked. "Ohhhh! Here's Grandpa's Angel! Who wants to hang Grandpa's Angel?!" So naturally, when we started this book, my first question to my mother was, "Where's Grandpa's Angel? You gotta send her up!" This page is dedicated to the loving memory of my grandfather, Roland S. Leh Sr. **-D**

As much as Christmas is for giving, it is also very much for eating, and no holiday table would dare be called complete without a set (or three) of festive **SALT 'N' PEPPER SHAKERS**. Embodying every theme, shape, and coupling imaginable, they are one of the few knickknacks that were meant to be handled and juggled on a daily basis. Mystery, speculation, and debate surround the number of holes, which seasoning goes in the one that has fewer, and why shakers from fifty years ago had much larger holes than those made more recently. Sadly, the natural corrosive action of salt combined with the poor quality of the "cold painting" techniques — not to mention the ravages brought about by the automatic dishwasher — explain why very few pristine examples remain. There is also the fact that when one of these little puppies broke, both of them usually ended up in the pail, although there does seem to be an abundance of merry orphans begging to be adopted at every tag, yard, and garage sale.

With the huge success of John Marks's song "Rudolph the Red-Nosed Reindeer" in 1949 (which remarkably sold a whopping 2 million records in its first season alone), Jack Nelson and Steve Rollins decided to try come up with a follow-up tune to ride on its lucrative coattails (or reindeer hooves). They tinkered with giving lots of wintry denizens new magical features, but really didn't hit upon anything worthy of pop adulation until they placed a silk hat on a pile of snow and it started to gyrate madly.

Presto-change-o! **FROSTY** was born! They raced their newly penned creation straight over to Gene Autry, who was more than willing to experience multiplatinum déjà vu in the upcoming holiday season. They even sold him "Here Comes Peter Cottontail" at the same time. Some talented songwriting duo those two made! While "Frosty the Snowman" didn't quite hit the sales of a certain reindeer's, the snowman himself has certainly become ingrained in the public psyche as a Christmas icon.

Wonderland

Each holiday season, my family would make a pilgrimage north to Lantana, Florida, to experience firsthand the wonders of the *National Enquirer* holidayland displays. It was a big deal: acres and acres of twinkling lights, animatronic scenes in all their candyland finery, and the "world's tallest decorated tree" for most of the 1970s. One year we made the hour-long journey in style in our neighbors' overly large recreational vehicle. They were collectors, and I distinctly remember how incredibly stuffed their "home on wheels" was with Christmas keepsakes. It made quite an impression on me. Snowy vignettes occupied every available flat surface, each one containing a plethora of **CERAMIC GIRLS**—resplendent with wings, innocent expresssions, and piles and piles of holiday offerings. Perhaps cramming eighteen people into the camper was not a great idea, or maybe it was the excess weight of all those knickknacks, but the RV sputtered to a grinding halt in a gas station parking lot about halfway there. My father—always eager to leap at the chance to make a scene—hauled out his ever-present boom box (with

"Christmas Jollies" by the SalSoul Orchestra blaring) and started doing a "Dr. Jam Strut" in large, looping circles. Difficult to describe, the dance is a cross between soul grooves, wild arm flailings, and a bit of German oompah-band leg squats thrown in for heredity's sake. Instead of blindly running away out of sheer embarrassment and wishing to be struck dead on the spot (which was the usual end result when venturing out into public with him), we all started clapping and joined in with his "clomping" right in front of a gathering crowd of nosy onlookers. It was the first time I realized what a true gift a free spirit could be, and what amazing, transformative powers Christmas carols could provide. **-D**

Little paraffin figure-candles were as much of an omnipresence during the holiday season as Santa himself. Their delicate, glossy, painted-on accents and snowy white "whipped-like-Crisco" appearance would cause me endless hours of speculation about just how good they must taste (I never tried, but Ralph claims there was not a single one in the Del Pozzo household lacking teeth marks). The candles were first made in the late 1930s when Socony-Vacuum Oil Company (now Exxon-Mobil) hired Franklin Gurley to create a line of decorative candles to help use up the extra paraffin, then a useless by-product of oil refining. They were sold in Woolworth's across the United States and in fancier stores like Macy's, under the name **TAVERN CANDLES**. It's amazing how well and how many of these delicate confections have held up. Although many were never burned to preserve their adorable appearance, they were most likely stored improperly. While the attic may seem like a good place to tuck away all your Christmas paraphernalia until the following season, the heat wreaks havoc on antique collectibles — peeling paints and stains, warping and discoloring plastics, and turning little paraffin people into nighmarish puddles.

CHICKENLICK AND THUMBNAIL SANTA just got pulled from the clutches of Frostbit Creek...they were drifting for days in nothing but a wreath float, in their cotton jammies! He got his name when he was born with a feather for hair, so "Cowlick" just didn't make sense. **-R**

CHRISTMAS SEALS

were started near Copenhagen in 1904 by a postman named Einar Holboell. Legend has it that he was struck by the difference between the goodwill of all holiday cards he was sorting and the hopeless look of two ragamuffins he momentarily glimpsed outside his office window. He created an extra Christmas "stamp," the procceeds of which would go toward helping needy children. Emily Bissell brought the seals to American shores in 1907 to raise funds for a children's tuberculosis shelter. At first she met great resistance, as many believed the disease was incurable and did not like the idea of linking it with Christmas. It was only after a Philadelphia columnist, Leigh Mitchell Hodges, jumped on board in his newspaper, *The North American*, that the idea really caught on. My fondest memory of Christmas seals was the year my cousin used them to découpage her entire desk — including the blotter and matching pen holder — for a quick, colorful, and super-cool makeover. **- D**

POLLYWOG BOY

slithered with glee. After years
of nothing but red slippers
and coal, he finally
got his black bunny. **-R**

actual size
of face:
half an inch

actual size
of pom-pom:
two inches

Those of us who celebrate Christmas all have one thing in common: that time in our life when we truly believed in the bearded super-hero. Greater than Superman, Batman, the Tooth Fairy, and all those other guys in tights put together — and he was real! Of course, as the years progressed, loose ends began to add up and things started to not ring true. The chimney? Flying? Wish lists from kids all over the world? And what about all those imposters at Christmas parties and Sears?

I don't think any of us can remember the exact moment we learned the true meaning of **KRIS KRINGLE**, simply because we prefer to collectively block it. For that was the very day we began our journey into adulthood and had to start facing the realities of life — including the pain of deceit caused by those we trusted the most. Good thing they camouflaged that deceit with lots of presents! **-R**

In 1939, Robert May, a copywriter for Montgomery Ward, was asked to write a promotional Christmas poem for the upcoming holiday season. He came up with **ROLLO THE RED-NOSED REINDEER**. Executives of the company liked the story, but weren't crazy about the name Rollo, feeling it was too "carefree" and "cheerful." The beleaguered reindeer was renamed **REGINALD**, which was also rejected, this time for sounding "too British." (Seems like the golden age of advertising was more similar to today's world than previously realized.) May wracked his brains trying to come up with another fictional reindeer name, but none quite fit — until his four-year-old daughter suggested **RUDOLPH**. The rest of the story, as the saying goes, is history.

Some say that May based his red-nosed reindeer rhyme, essentially a reworking of **THE UGLY DUCKLING**, on his own childhood experiences as a small and shy outcast. Incredibly, Rudy's most famous asset, his glowing proboscis, was first met with great hesitation on the part of the Montgomery Ward higher-ups. They felt that its associations with drunkenness and debauchery might prove inappropriate for a children's holiday story. May then enlisted the help of Denver Gillen, a work associate from the art department, to accompany him to the Lincoln Park Zoo to sketch deer. The resulting drawings, with noses all aglow, finally netted the project full approval.

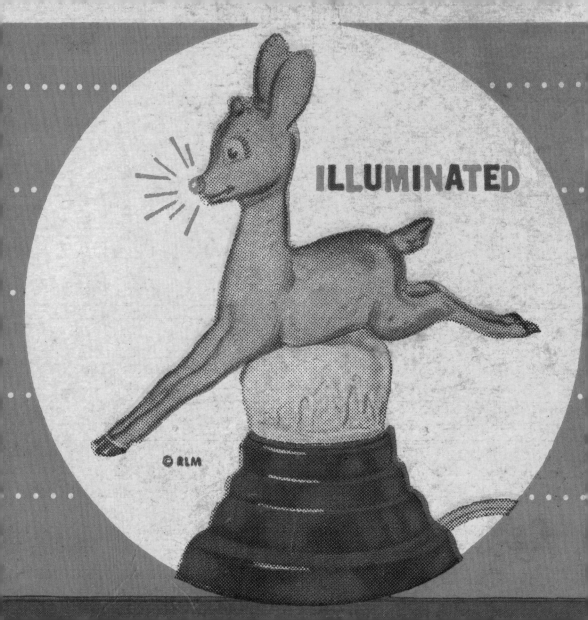

ILLUMINATED

© RLM

These little plastic prancers were originally attached to a cardboard disk with a hole in the center and marketed alongside the children's record "Rudolph the Red-Nosed Reindeer." They were meant to be placed on the turntable, on top of the record, so Rudy could spin 'round and 'round the whole time the record played.

The earliest artificial Christmas trees were from Germany and made out of goose feathers and animal hair. In 1883, Sears, Roebuck & Co. offered a 33-limbed tree for only 50 cents and a 55-limbed deluxe model for a mere dollar. Real trees began to be sold commercially in the United States around 1851 and were taken randomly from natural forests. People didn't consider this to be "stealing" back then, and timberland was plentiful. By the early 1900s, however, overharvesting of the evergreens and decimation of fir groves began to alarm conservationists. Theodore Roosevelt even tried to eliminate the role of Christmas trees from holiday celebrations in 1901. Around the same time, the first artificial trees were manufactured in the United States by the Addis Brush Company, which also manufactured toilet bowl brushes. These came to be known as **BOTTLE BRUSH TREES** (which had a much nicer ring to it than "toilet-brush trees"). That same year, the first commercial tree farm was started by W.V. McGalliard, who planted 25,000 Norway spruces on his New Jersey farmstead. Now there are approximately 500,000 acres dedicated to Christmas tree farming in the United States alone, with each acre producing enough oxygen to meet the daily requirements of roughly eighteen people.

Did you ever receive a **GIFT** so completely bizarre that you just couldn't fathom how the giver could possibly think you would actually *like* it? Reminds me of the story a good friend told me from her teens when a distant relative, a knitter, came bearing gifts. The woman had brought along her young son who was proudly gilt in a patchwork vest knit in a plethora of colors, from earth browns to hot pinks to avocado greens. Just the sight of the kid in his cross-stitch calamity provided enough comic relief to make the concept of "holiday visiting" seem almost bearable for her — until she opened her own gift and discovered a perfect match. Worse than the gift itself was the realization that she would have to wear it with a smile for the rest of the day. Moments like these teach us how to put on our best face during times of extreme emotional duress. **-R**

over the years those holiday cheers
would return with a
sparkling vengeance.

the tree's heaving needles
and leans towards the nail.
sweet angel is crooked,
the forecast warns: hail!

the bulb is burned out
and so are the cookies.
yet it all seems so
wonderfully warm this year,
it all seems so wonderfully warm.

-R

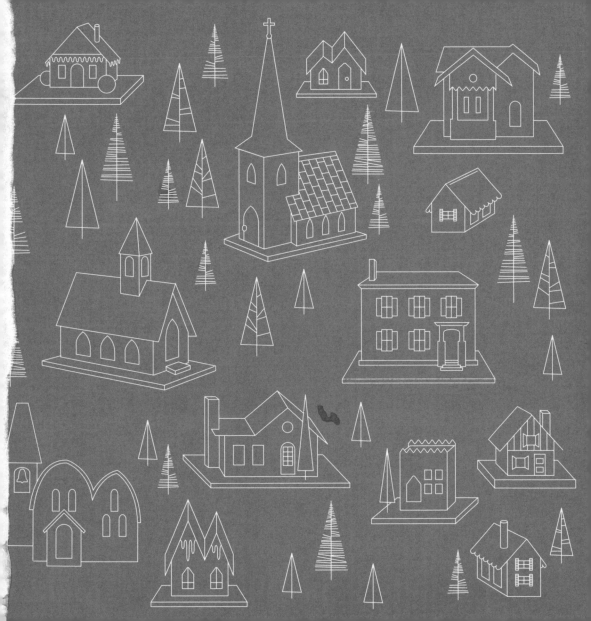

FINIS